Crescent City, U.S.A.
April 7, 2013
クレセントシティー
２０１３年4月7日

東日本大震災で流された岩手県立高田高校のボートが震災の二年後にアメリカ合衆国カルフォルニア州のクレセントシティーで見つかった事から始まったこの二校の交流は両国の多くの方々のおかげで可能になりました。在日アメリカ大使館のキャロライン　ケネディ大使、ジョン　ルース前米国大使、TOMODACHIイニシャティブ、米日財団、米国国立海洋大気庁、在米サンフランシスコ日本総領事館、日本郵船会社の皆様、出版にあたって指導してくださった方々、デルノーテ高校の校長と先生と生徒たち、高田高校の校長と先生と生徒たち、デルノーテ群の住民、陸前高田市の市民、陸前高田市役所職員、編集に協力してくださった方、そして作者の家族に心から感謝いたします。

Illustration and book design: Amy Uyeki
Photo credits: p. 43: Bryant Anderson/Del Norte Triplicate, p. 44: Amya Miller
Published by Humboldt State University Press
First and third printing by Bug Press in Arcata, California, U.S.A, 2015, 2016
Second printing by Niinuma Kikaku Insatsu in Ofunato, Japan, 2016

Dengler, Lori and Miller, Amya
The Extraordinary Voyage of Kamome
A Tsunami Boat Comes Home
46 p.
ISBN 978-0-9966731-0-5
Summary: A tsunami boat brings hope and friendship
to two communities on opposite sides of the ocean
Tsunamis–Japan–Juvenile non-fiction
Earthquakes–Juvenile non-fiction
Cultural exchange–Juvenile non-fiction
With historical references, guide to talking to children about disaster preparedness

A note on the text: The Japanese and English versions are not exact translations. Each tell the story of Kamome with considerations for the cultural sensitivities of each audience.

The return of Kamome, the exchanges between Del Norte and Takata High Schools, and this book would not be possible without the support of many individuals and agencies. We thank Mary O'Reilly, R.N., the Desert Community Foundation, the Mia-Bo Fund of the Humboldt Area Foundation, and the California State Tsunami Program for providing funding to complete this book.

The initial retrieval and identification of the boat was made by the efforts of the Del Norte County Sheriff's Department, the Redwood Coast Tsunami Work Group, the U.S. National Oceanographic and Atmospheric Administration (NOAA), Troy Nicolini, Sherry Lippiatt, Keeley Belva, and Kumi Watanabe-Shock. Marine species were identified by HSU Biology Professor Sean Craig. The return of the boat was initiated by Del Norte students, teacher Joyce Ruiz, Principal Coleen Parker and Del Norte Sheriff's Deputy Bill Stevens. Nippon Yusen Kaisha provided resources to return Kamome to Japan.

We extend our gratitude to Her Excellency Ambassador Caroline Kennedy of the U.S. Embassy in Japan, Acting Consul General Nobuhiro Watanabe and the Consulate-General of Japan in San Francisco, His Excellency former Ambassador John Roos, the TOMODACHI Initiative, the U.S.-Japan Council, and all of the Rikuzentakata City Hall employees without whose support the exchange between the two high schools would not be possible. We thank Malcolm Margolin and Robin Renshaw for their editorial suggestions, Cyril Oberlander and Robert Arena for their invaluable advice regarding this publication. We acknowledge all of the people in Rikuzentakata, Japan and Crescent City, California who eagerly embraced the story of Kamome and have supported the connections between these two cities. We thank our friends and family members whose encouragement and suggestions have been invaluable.

To all of the children in Japan and elsewhere in the Pacific who were affected by the 2011 Japan tsunami.

Humboldt State University Press
Library
1 Harpst St.
Arcata, CA 95521-8299

THE EXTRAORDINARY VOYAGE OF KAMOME

A Tsunami Boat Comes Home

Written by Lori Dengler and Amya Miller
Designed and Illustrated by Amy Uyeki

日本の
とうほくちほうに
りくぜんたかた
という
小さな町が
あります。
海と山が
きれいな町です。

There is a place called Rikuzentakata in Japan near the beautiful Pacific Ocean. The people love their high mountains, beaches, and tall pine trees.

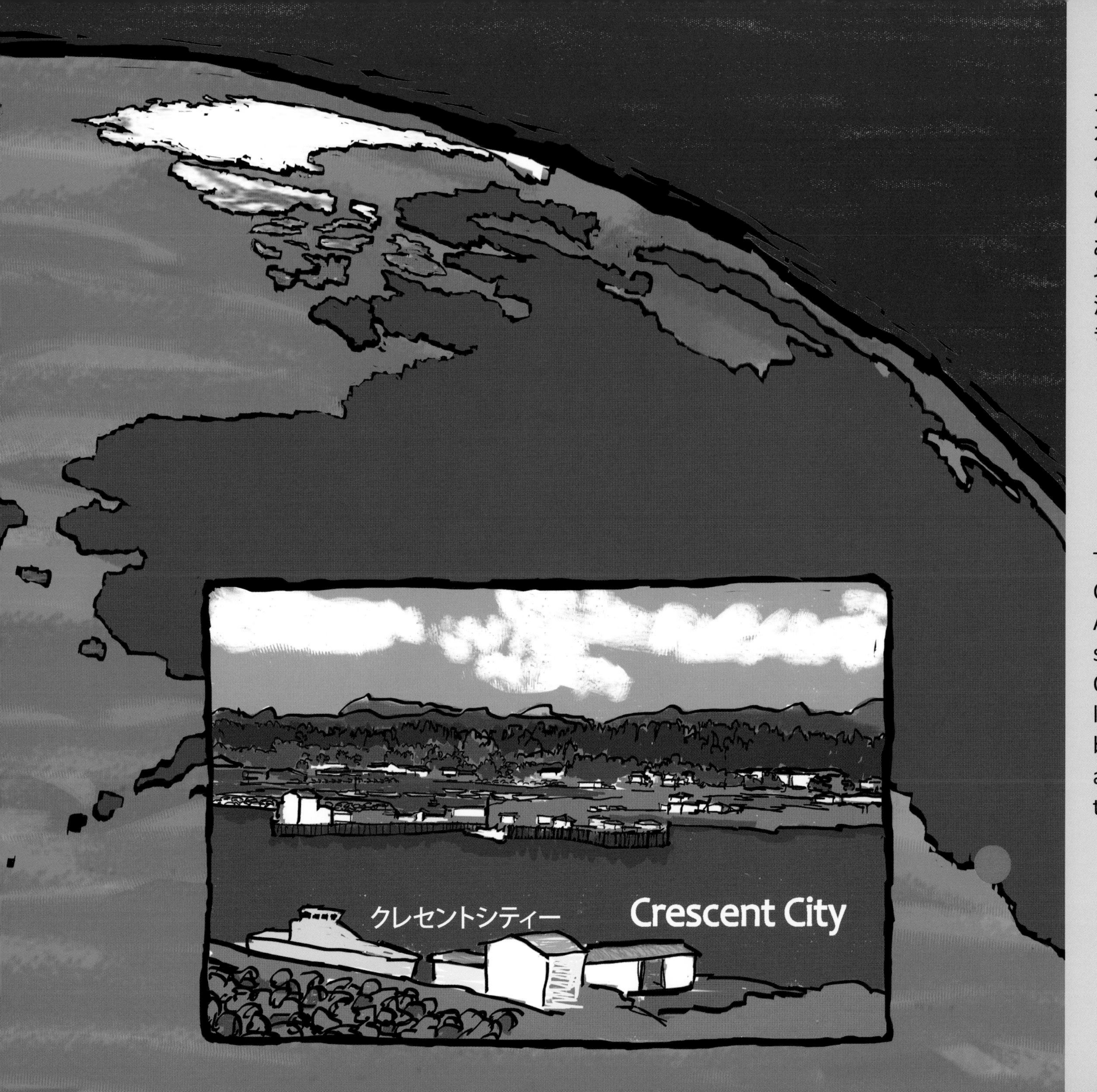

アメリカの
カルフォルニアしゅうに
クレセントシティー
という
小さな町が
あります。
そこも
海と山が
きれいな町です。

There is a place called Crescent City in America on the other side of the Pacific Ocean. The people love their beautiful beaches, mountains, and giant redwood trees.

りくぜんたかたには
先生
りょうしさん
けいさつかん
コックさん
お父さんたちと
お母さんたちが
すんでいます。
こどもも
おとしよりも
すんでいます。

Who lives in Rikuzentakata? There are grandparents, mothers, fathers, teenagers, and young children. The grownups have many different jobs. Some are teachers, police officers, firefighters, and chefs. Some work on boats and fish and others have jobs that help their city.

クレセントシティーにも
いろんな人が
すんでいます。
こども
こうこうせい
お母さんたち
お父さんたち
おばあちゃん
おじいちゃんも
すんでいます。
この町にも
りょうしさんや
先生
コックさん
けいさつかんがいます。

Families live in Crescent City, too. There are small children and teenagers and mothers and fathers and grand-parents. People work as fishermen, teachers, chefs, police officers, firefighters and at many other jobs.

りくぜんたかたには
こうこうが
ありました。
たかたこうこう
という学校です。
この学校の
せいとたちは
みんな
えいごを
べんきょうしていました。
アメリカの
こともべんきょう
していたのですが
クレセントシティー
というなまえの町は
だれもきいたことが
なかったのです。

There is a school in Rikuzentakata called Takata High School. Here, Japanese teenagers know that America is very far away and that the people speak a different language and eat different foods. The students had never heard of Crescent City.

クレセントシティーにも
こうこうがあります。
デルノーテこうこう
という学校です。
この学校の
せいとたちは
日本は
海のはんたいがわに
あるところだと
まなんでいました。
でもりくぜんたかた
というなまえの町は
だれもきいたことが
なかったのです。

There is a school in Crescent City called Del Norte High School. American teenagers there know that Japan is on the other side of the ocean, and that the people speak another language and eat different food. They had never heard of Rikuzentakata and couldn't imagine going to such a far away place.

たかたこうこうの
せいとたちは
海について
べんきょうを
するために
ボートを
つかっていました。
せいとたちは
このボートに
「高田高校」と
マジックで学校の
なまえをかいたのです。

Takata High School had a little boat to help students learn about the ocean and how to fish. It was named "Kamome," the Japanese word for seagull. They painted "Takata High School" on the side so that everyone would know it was their boat.

これが
かんじの
なまえです。

The characters
looked like this:

高田高校

ある日
とうほくちほうに
大きなじしんが
きました。
そのあと
大きなつなみも
きたのです。
つなみで
りくぜんたかたの
たくさんのたてものや
車やふねが
ながされました。

One day there was a very big earthquake. The ground shook and shook and shook. The earthquake caused big waves called a tsunami. The tsunami swept over the city of Rikuzentakata and washed many buildings, cars, and boats into the ocean. The people were frightened and angry and sad.

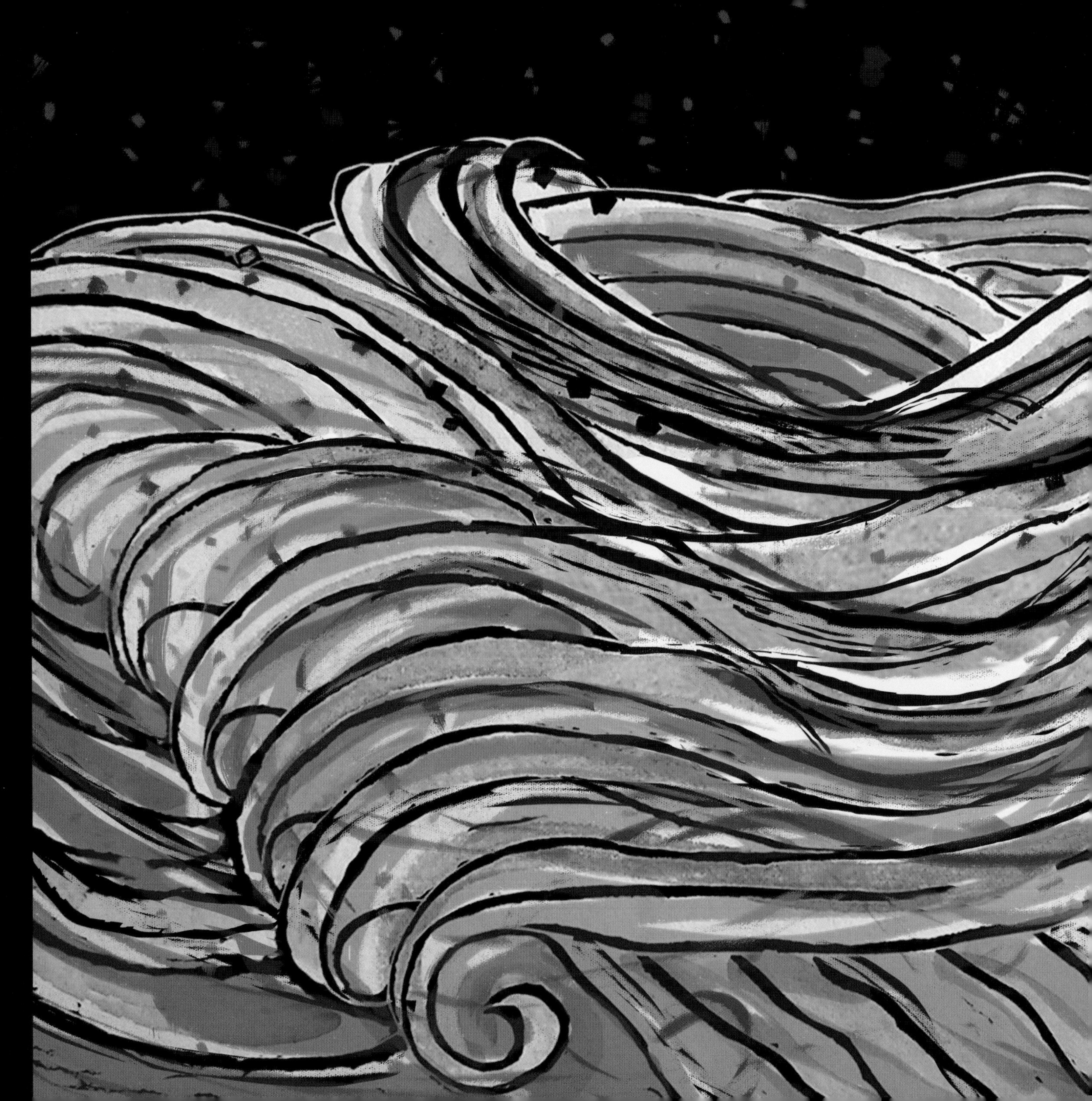

日本で
おきたじしんで
アメリカにも
つなみがきました。
クレセントシティーに
つなみが
きたときは
りくぜんたかたの
つなみよりも
ちいさかったのですが
それでも
たくさんのふねが
ながされてしまいました。

The tsunami traveled all the way across the Pacific Ocean to America. By the time it reached Crescent City, it was much smaller, but was still big enough to sweep over the harbor in Crescent City and sink many boats.

たかたこうこうの
せいとが
つかっていた
ボートも
つなみで
ながされて
しまいました。
ボートは
たいへいように
むかって
ながれていったのです。

Kamome and the
other boats were
washed out into the
ocean by the big
tsunami waves.
Kamome was carried
far, far off the coast.
The people thought
the little boat and
all the other things
caught in the tsunami
were lost forever.

つなみで
ボートは
ひっくりかえって
さかさまに
なりました。
ボートは
ずっと
たいへいようを
わたっていきました。

The big tsunami waves flipped Kamome upside down. The only part of the little boat above the water was her blue bottom. The winds and the ocean slowly pushed Kamome away from Japan and towards America.

かぜとなみで
アメリカに
むかって
ながれていきました。

Kamome was alone in
the big Pacific Ocean.

あるときには
ボートは
大きなあらしに
まきこまれることも
ありました。

Sometimes Kamome
was caught in big
storms that tossed
the little boat back
and forth, up and
down. Great waves
splashed completely
over her. But the littl
boat was very strong
and kept on floating.

ボートが
海を
わたっていた
ときには
とりや
くじらや
いるかや
さかなが
見にきました。
「これは
なんだろう」と
おもったのでしょう。

The little boat's only companions were sea birds, whales, dolphins, fish, and other sea creatures.

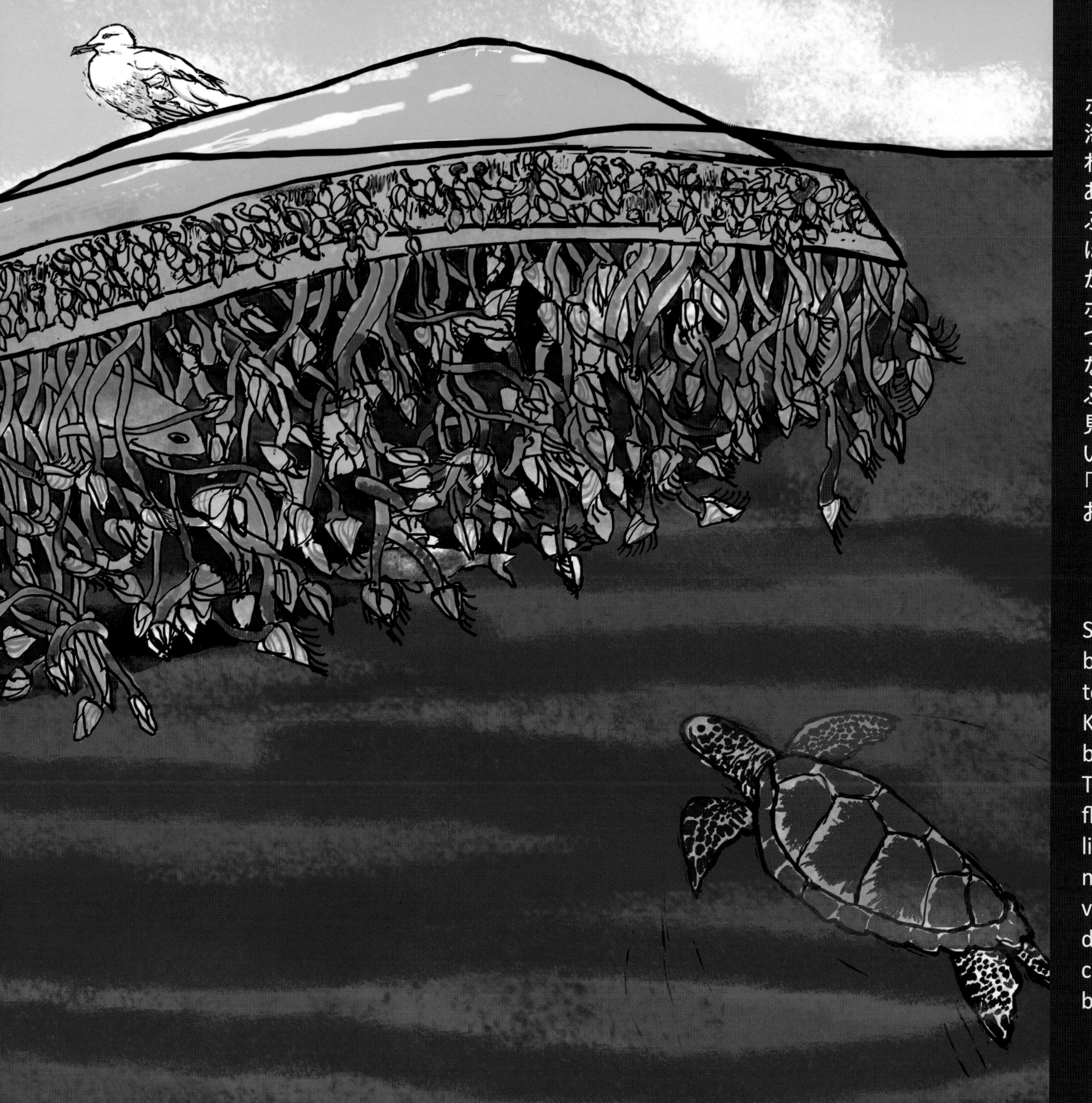

ボートが
海を
わたっていた
あいだに
ふじつぼという
ほそながい
かいが
ボートに
ついていきました。
ながくなっていった
ふじつぼを
見ていた
いるかたちは
「これもなんだろう」と
おもったのでしょう。

Sea animals called
barnacles stuck
to every part of
Kamome that was
beneath the water.
Their long necks
floated beneath the
little boat. Kamome
must have looked
very strange to the
dolphins and other
creatures that swam
beneath her.

ふじつぼは
どんどんながく
なっていきました。
ボートの下に
ふとい
うどんのように
なっていったのです。
なんかげつも
なんかげつも
じかんがたちました。
このあいだに
日本では
お正月が二回
おいわいされました。

The barnacles grew and grew until they were more than a foot long, dangling beneath the boat like big noodles.

Months and months went by. The New Year came and went and came again.

つなみで町が
なくなってしまった
りくぜんたかたの
人は　さびしい
きもちが
つづきました。
でも　アメリカでは
りくぜんたかたで
おきたつなみは
とおいむかしの
できごとだったので
みんな
わすれていたのです。

It was hard for the people in Rikuzen-takata to enjoy New Year's celebrations like making mochi. Most of their beautiful town was gone and they were reminded of the terrible tsunami every day .

In America, many people had forgotten about the tsunami and what had happened in Japan.

つなみがおきた
二年ご
かわったかたちの
ボートが
クレセントシティーに
たどりつきました。
このようなふねを
見たことがない
おおぜいの
アメリカ人が
ふねを
見にきました。
ボートのまわりには
ながいふじつぼが
たくさん
ついていました。

One day more than two years after the tsunami, a strange little boat washed ashore near Crescent City. The Americans had never seen a boat like this before. The long barnacles completely covered the sides.

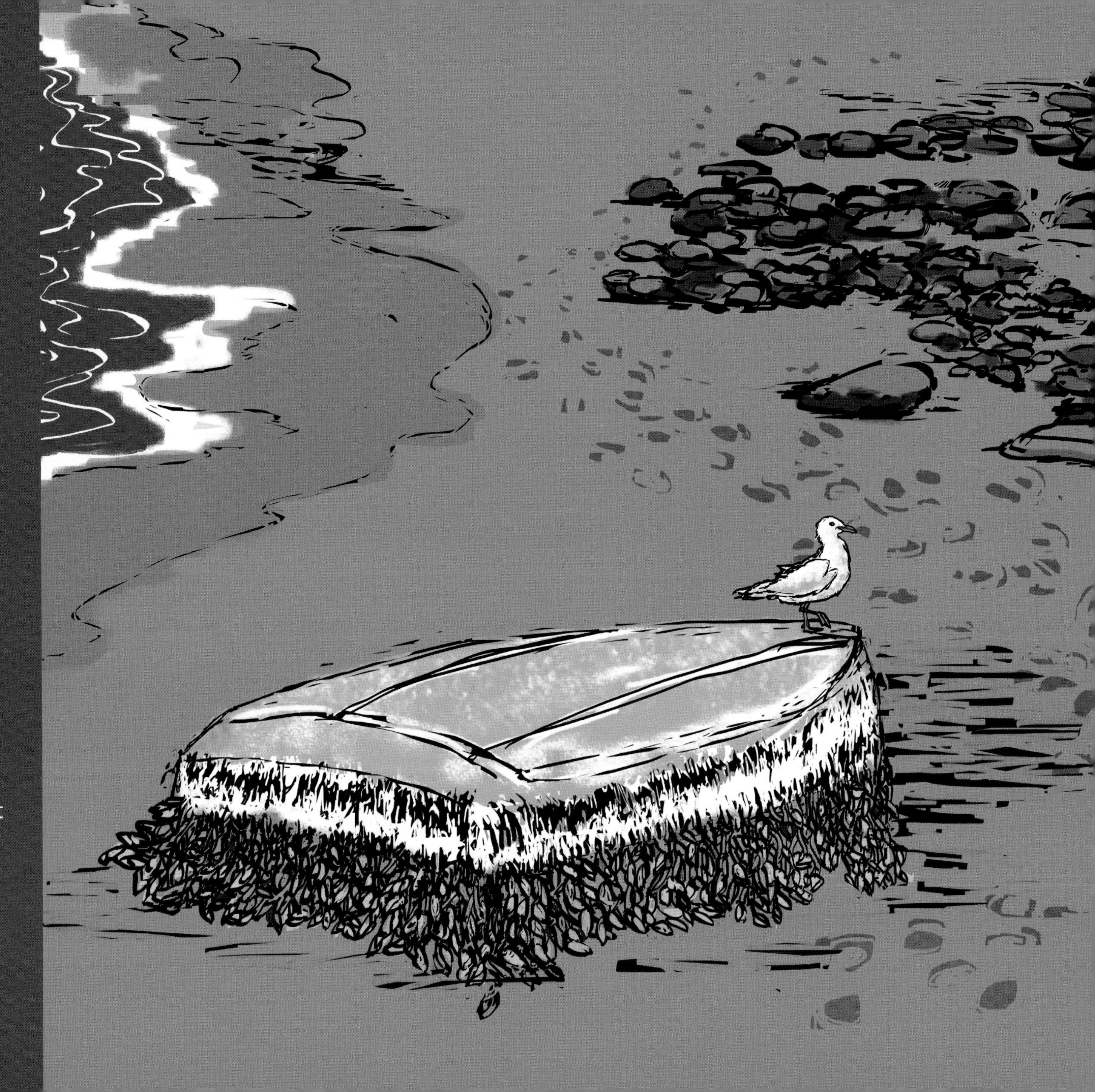

クレセントシティーに
ながれついたボートを
見にきた人は
「ふじつぼの下に
もじがあるよ」と
きづきました。

Many people came to look at the boat. They scraped some of the barnacles off the boat and saw the Japanese writing. They wondered what it said.

ふじつぼを
けずりおとして
「高田高校」
という字を
見つけたのです。
クレセントシティーの
人々は
たかたこうこうは
りくぜんたかたにあると
わかりこれは
つなみで
ながされたものだと
しりました。

A Japanese person read the characters which said "Takata High School. " The people in Crescent City learned that Takata High School was in Rikuzentakata, Japan and that the boat had been lost in the tsunami.

クレセントシティーの
デルノーテこうこうの
せいともボートを
見にきました。
ボートが
たいへいようを
わたったことに
おどろきました。

The students from Del Norte High School saw the boat, too. They were amazed that the little boat hadn’t sunk. They liked the name, Kamome, because there were a lot of seagulls in Crescent City.

ある日
デルノーテこうこうの
せいとがいいました。
「ボートを
きれいにして
かえしてあげよう。
つなみで
たくさんのものを
なくしてしまったので
ボートがかえって
くるとよろこぶかもね。」

No one knew what to do with the little boat. For weeks and weeks the little boat sat alone. One day the Del Norte High School students said, "Maybe we could send this boat back to the people who lost it."

デルノーテこうこうの
せいとたちは
ふねをきれいにして
それから
先生に
どうしたらふねを
りくぜんたかたに
かえせるかを
ききました。

The students cleaned the boat.

They talked to their teachers about how to send the boat home.

先生は
日本と
アメリカの
せいふの人と
りくぜんたかたの
しやくしょの人と
はなしを
しました。

The teachers talked to officials in America and Japan. Many people wanted to help return the little boat.

大きなふねを
もっている
会社の人が
「ボートを日本に
もっていってあげるよ。」
といってくれました。
ボートは大きな
ふねにのせられ
りくぜんたかたに
かえされることに
なりました。

Finally, Kamome was put on a ship to return to Japan.

It had taken the little boat two years to travel to America. The big ship took less than a week to take Kamome back to Japan!

ボートは
りくぜんたかたに
もどってきました。
たかたこうこうの
せいとたちは
このボートを
見にきました。
そしてボートに
「おかえり」
といいました。
うれしかったのです。

Takata High School students came out to see the little boat when she arrived in Rikuzentakata. It made the students smile to see their boat again.

たかたこうこうの
せいとと先生は
デルノーテこうこうの
せいとたちが
ボートを
りくぜんたかたに
かえしてくれた
おれいに
このせいとたちを
日本に
しょうたいしました。

Takata High School students and teachers were very thankful that the American students had worked so hard to send their boat back. They invited the American students to visit them in Japan.

でも
デルノーテこうこうの
せいとたちは
ちょっとだけ
こわかったのです。
日本ごも
はなせません。
日本のたべものも
たべたことが
ありません。
日本のたべものを
たべられるのか。
たかたこうこうの
せいとと
ともだちになれるのか。
デルノーテこうこうの
せいとは
ふあんでした。

The American teenagers were a little scared to go to Japan. They had never traveled so far away before. They didn't speak Japanese and wondered what it would be like to eat Japanese food and if the Japanese students would like them.

それでも
「たかたこうこうの
せいとにあいたい」
といって
ひこうきにのって
たいへいようをわたり
りくぜんたかたに
いくために
しんかんせんに
のったのです。
デルノーテこうこうの
せいとたちは
ようやく
たかたこうこうに
つきました。
かえってきた
ボートも
見にいきました。

They flew in an airplane across the Pacific Ocean and took a bullet train to Rikuzentakata. They visited Takata High School and met the Japanese teenagers. The American students were happy to see Kamome in Japan.

デルノーテこうこうの
せいとたちは
日本のごはんをつくり
日本のうたをうたい
自分のなまえを
かんじで
かいたりしました。
みんな
ニコニコと
わらっていました。

The American students learned to cook Japanese food and discovered it tasted good. They learned to sing a folk song and write their names in Japanese characters.

Everyone smiled and laughed.

りくぜんたかたの
人は
せいとたちが
たのしんでいる
すがたを見て
うれしかったのです。
アメリカのせいとが
かえるじかんに
なりました。
「こんどはアメリカで
あおうね」と
やくそくをしました。

The people in
Rikuzentakata were
happy to see the
students having fun.
When it was time
for the American
students to leave,
they asked their new
friends to visit them
in Crescent City.

一年が
たちました。
こんどは
たかたこうこうの
せいとたちが
ひこうきにのり
たいへいようをわたり
デルノーテこうこうに
いきました。

The next year, students from Takata High School got on an airplane and flew across the Pacific Ocean to America. They visited Crescent City and the students from Del Norte High School.

でも
たかたこうこうの
せいとたちも
ちょっとだけ
こわかったのです。
「がっこうでえいごを
べんきょうして
いるけれど
つうじるかな」
としんぱいでした。
アメリカのごはんは
おいしいのか。
デルノーテこうこうの
せいとと
ともだちになれるのか。
たかたこうこうの
せいとはふあんでした。

The Japanese students had never been to America. They studied English in school but were a little scared about talking to the Del Norte High School students and eating American food. They wondered if the American students would like them.

アメリカに
ついた
たかたこうこうの
せいとは
大きな
松の木を
見にいったり
ボートが
見つかった
かいがんに
いったりしました。

The Takata High School students saw the big redwood trees. They visited the spot where Kamome had washed ashore. The Japanese students and the American students laughed together.

アメリカの
うたを
うたったり
レストランで
えいごで
ちゅうもんしたり
しました。
アメリカと日本の
こうこうせいが
わらっているのを見て
クレセントシティーの
人は
うれしかったのです。

The Japanese students learned to sing an American song and write their names in English. They went to a restaurant and ate American food. Seeing the American and Japanese students laughing together made the people in Crescent City happy.

このボートの
おかげで
日本と
アメリカの
こうこうせいが
ともだちに
なれたのです。
たかたこうこうと
デルノーテこうこうの
せいとは
やくそくしました。
「いつまでもともだちで
いようね。」

What an amazing little boat! She survived the tsunami, traveled all the way across the ocean and then came back to Japan. Everywhere Kamome went, she made people happy.

The students from Takata High School and Del Norte High School made a pledge to each other. “Let’s be friends forever.”

For Parents and Educators

On April 7, 2013, a little over two years after a magnitude 9.0 earthquake triggered a massive tsunami off the coast of north-eastern Japan, a lone boat washed up on the shores of Crescent City, California. Humboldt State University Geology Professor Lori Dengler was one of the experts called in to examine the boat. Dr. Dengler contacted Amya Miller, the Director of Global Public Relations for Rikuzentakata, beginning the process of linking the boat to Takata High School.

The Japanese Consulate in San Francisco and the National Oceanic and Atmospheric Administration declared the boat as tsunami debris, lost in the disaster of March 11, 2011. At the time of the tsunami, Kamome was tied up in a storage area. No one was in the boat.

Students at Del Norte High School in Crescent City, California cleaned the boat and worked with Amya Miller to find resources to return the boat. On October 21, 2013, 954 days after it was pulled away by the tsunami, the boat returned to Rikuzentakata.

Kamome has become a symbol of resilience, hope, and dialogue. Amya Miller worked with both Takata High School and Del Norte High School administrators, staff, and students, to forge a formal sister school partnership. In February 2014, Del Norte High School students visited Rikuzentakata, and in January 2015, Takata High School students visited Del Norte County, California.

The bonds formed between the students and the communities have transformed the lives of people in Rikuzentakata and Crescent City. One boat and its voyage across the Pacific Ocean and back to Japan has resulted in two very different high schools and communities committed to friendship.

In 2014, Kamome was moved to the National Tokyo Museum as a special exhibit on the 2011 tsunami and Japanese recovery. Kamome's voyage has triggered a new wave. It is our hope this new wave leads to happiness, awareness, and hope for all people who read this story.

Visit humboldt.edu/kamome for more information and photos about the extraordinary voyage of Kamome.

Del Norte High students write their names in Japanese

ボートから始まった交流

この本は実話に基づいて書かれたものです。東日本大震災の約２年後の２０１３年４月７日にアメリカのカルフォルニア州のクレセントシティーの海岸に一隻のボートが漂着しました。ハンボルト大学の地理学の専門家、ローリー　デングラー教授はボートに関する調査をしにクレセントシティーに４月７日に向かいました。デングラー教授は陸前高田市の当時海外広報ディレクターであったアミア　ミラーさんに連絡を取り、ボートが陸前高田市の高田高校のものであると知りました。

在米サンフランシスコ日本領事館と米国海洋大気庁が正式にこのボートは震災で流されたものであると判明しました。クレセントシティーの地元の高校生からボートを陸前高田に返したいとの声が上がり、生徒たちは陸前高田市役所のミラーさんと一緒にどのようにボートを返せるかの交渉を始めました。震災の９５４日後にボートはクレセントシティーを立ち、陸前高田に向かいました。

このボートは希望と奇跡と絆のシンボルになりました。ミラーさんは高田高校とデルノーテ高校との話し合いを始め、長期的な交流の為の金銭的な支援を手配しました。２０１４年の２月にはデルノーテ高校の生徒が陸前高田へ、２０１５年１月には高田高校の生徒がクレセントシティーに行くなど、交流が深まっています。

ボートは２０１５年３月に国立博物館に展示され、震災に関する教訓と交流を説明するものにもなりました。

震災がもたらした悲劇から生まれた奇跡はこれからも陸前高田市とクレセントシティーをつなげる架け橋になります。この実話を世界の子供に知ってもらい、防災教育に活用して頂きたいと思います。

ご父母、教師の方々へ

東日本大震災で亡くなられた方のご冥福をお祈りすると共に被害を受けられた方々と共に1日も早い復興を願います。

震災がもたらした悲惨な映像は世界各地で多くの方々が見られたものでしょう。また、２０１１年３月１１日の地震は日本ではもちろん、津波は太平洋のあらゆるところで起きました。自然がもたらす災害が多い日本では日頃から避難訓練などが学校で行われています。東日本大震災だけではなく、洪水、火山の噴火、地震などの映像や写真はテレビでもインターネットでも見られます。被災地の東北地方だけではなく、日本全国で放送された東日本大震災に関する映像は子供にとっては怖いものです。では、子供を対象にどのように過去に起きた、またこれから起きるであろう震災の事を話すべきなのでしょうか。

防災教育は国によって、文化の違いによって異なります。アメリカの防災教育は必ずしも日本では通用しません。この本の内容も文化の違いに基づいて文章を変えていますので、英語と日本語の文章には少々違いがあります。特に、被災地に住んでいる子供達のメンタルヘルスケアを意識し、津波で当然人も流された事は意図的に書かない事にしました。

アメリカでは感情を表に出し、家族と、学校内で、また友達同士で気持ちを表した防災教育が重視されています。子供が抱く恐怖感をなくす事はできません。でも、アメリカでは事前に「地震が来たらどうするか」、また「津波が来たらどうするか」の話し合いは必要だと思われています。子供の気持ちを把握し、家族で、または学校で避難についての情報と手段を与える事によって万が一の時をどう非難すべきなのかが分かるであろう。そして話し合っていく事によって子供達も恐怖感が和らぐだろうと思われています。

事前に出来る事とは、

•避難訓練の際に子供に責任感を持たせる行動が何かを話し合う。机の下にしゃがんで地震の揺れが収まるのを待つだけではなく、泣いている子供を励ますとか、津波から逃げる際には泣いてもいいからとにかく手をつないで怖がっている友達と走る。
子供の視線から見て考えるのも良いでしょう。
•家族ぐるみの避難訓練も行いましょう。どこにどうやって逃げるのかはご家族の方と一緒に練習する事によって体も慣れますし、安全に避難できる確率が高まります。
•子供の小さなリュックに避難する際に持っていきたいものを事前に準備し、「逃げる時にはこれを持っていってね」と、話し合いましょう。子供が好きなぬいぐるみ、絵本、おかしなどがあれば避難してからも気持ちが落ち着きます。

地震、津波、竜巻、火山の噴火などのテレビの映像などは子供がいるところでは見ない事をお勧めします。特に、東日本大震災の生々しい映像は未だに子供達にとっては怖いものです。

作者はこの本を通して子供とどう防災に関する話をするかを考えるきっかけになる事を期待します。意識を高め、知識を深めて話し合うことによって、また世界のどこかで起きる自然が齎す災害から身を守ることが出来る事を願います。

Talking to Young Children about Disasters

Psychologists believe that children can cope more effectively with a disaster when they know there are things they and their family can do to keep safe. Providing age-appropriate information will help them to understand what might happen and lessen their anxiety if a disaster does occur.

Involve your children in the process of preparing.

- Practice "Drop, Cover, and Hold On" drills at home or at schools or preschools. Count out how long your pretend earthquake lasts — a great way to learn numbers and a help to stay calm when a real earthquake strikes.

- Do an earthquake safety hunt in your home. Look for things that might fall or slide. Your children might spot things you haven't noticed.

- Work with your child to put together a personal kit. Talk about what items should be in the kit and let your child choose a stuffed toy, a blanket or a favorite book.

- Hold family tsunami evacuation drills. After you have done the drill a few times, let your children lead the way. The more you practice, the more familiar the process will become.

Let children know the steps that are being taken by you and your community to keep them safe. Children can sense topics you are uncomfortable discussing — the better prepared you are and the more willing you are to answer any questions they may have, the more secure they will feel.

After disaster strikes, limit media coverage of the disaster — if children are going to watch television or video material, consider taping it and previewing the material. Then watch it with them so you can answer questions and help them process the information. Children (and adults) don't benefit from graphic details or repeated exposure to disturbing images or sounds. The aftermath of a crisis is a good time to disconnect from all media and sit down together and talk as a family.

We hope that this book will provide a first step in talking with your children about disasters. For more information you can visit the website: humboldt.edu/kamome.

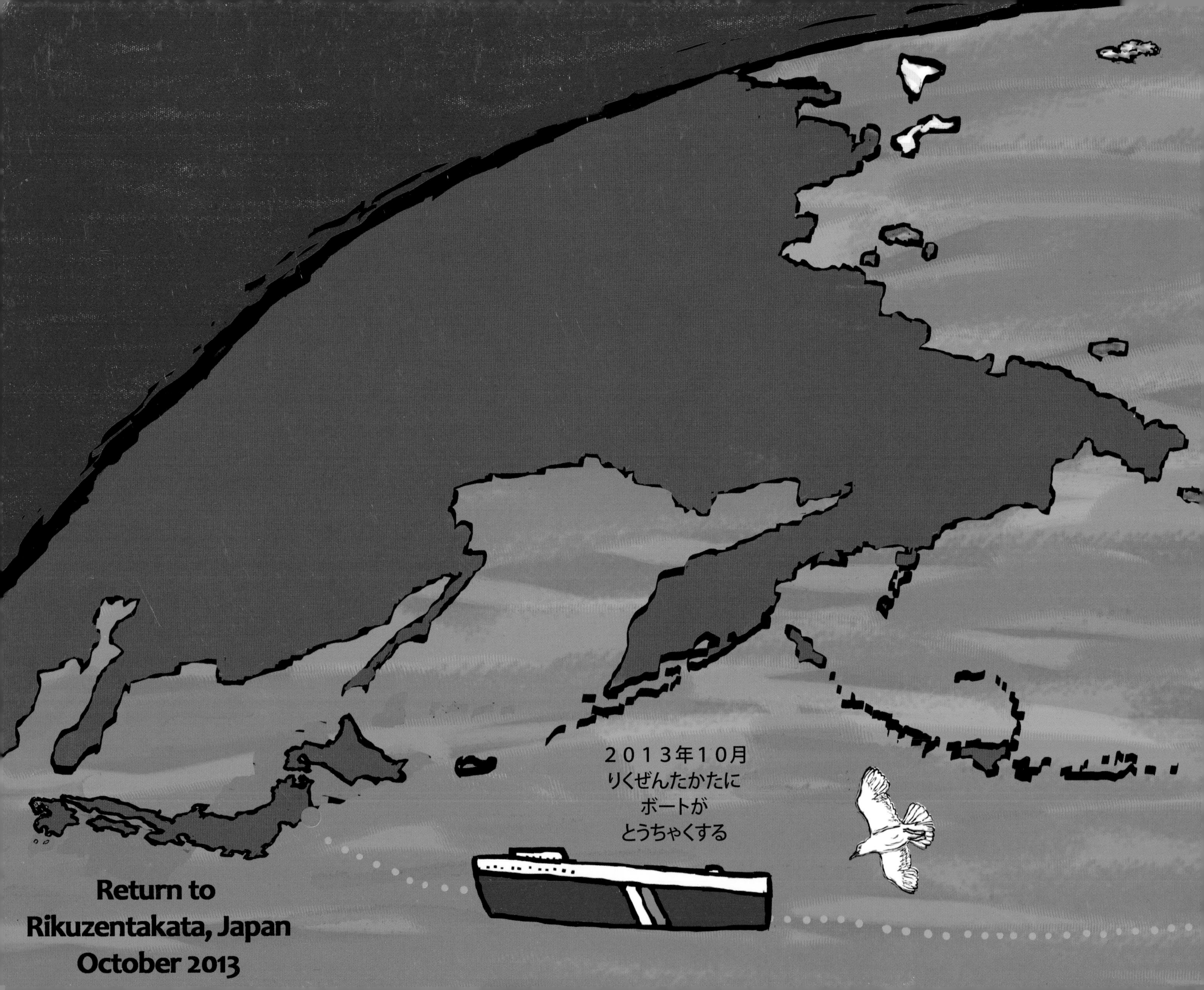

２０１３年１０月
りくぜんたかたに
ボートが
とうちゃくする
Return to
Rikuzentakata, Japan
October 2013